THE WORLD OF DINOSAURS

VELOCIRAPTOR

BY REBECCA SABELKO

EPIC

BELLWETHER MEDIA • MINNEAPOLIS, MN

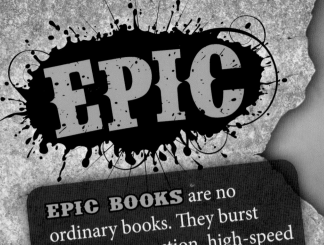

EPIC BOOKS are no ordinary books. They burst with intense action, high-speed heroics, and shadows of the unknown. Are you ready for an Epic adventure?

This edition first published in 2020 by Bellwether Media, Inc.

No part of this publication may be reproduced in whole or in part without written permission of the publisher. For information regarding permission, write to Bellwether Media, Inc., Attention: Permissions Department, 6012 Blue Circle Drive, Minnetonka, MN 55343.

Library of Congress Cataloging-in-Publication Data

Names: Sabelko, Rebecca, author.
Title: Velociraptor / by Rebecca Sabelko.
Description: Minneapolis, MN : Bellwether Media, Inc., [2020] | Series: Epic: The World of Dinosaurs | Audience: Ages 7-12. | Audience: Grades 2 to 7. | Includes bibliographical references and index.
Identifiers: LCCN 2019002816 (print) | LCCN 2019009548 (ebook) |
  ISBN 9781618916631 (ebook) | ISBN 9781644870914 (hardcover : alk. paper) |
  ISBN 9781618917386 (pbk. : alk. paper)
Subjects: LCSH: Velociraptor--Juvenile literature. | Dinosaurs--Juvenile literature.
Classification: LCC QE862.S3 (ebook) | LCC QE862.S3 S23255 2020 (print) | DDC 567.912--dc23
LC record available at https://lccn.loc.gov/2019002816

Editor: Betsy Rathburn   Designer: Jeffrey Kollock

Printed in the United States of America, North Mankato, MN

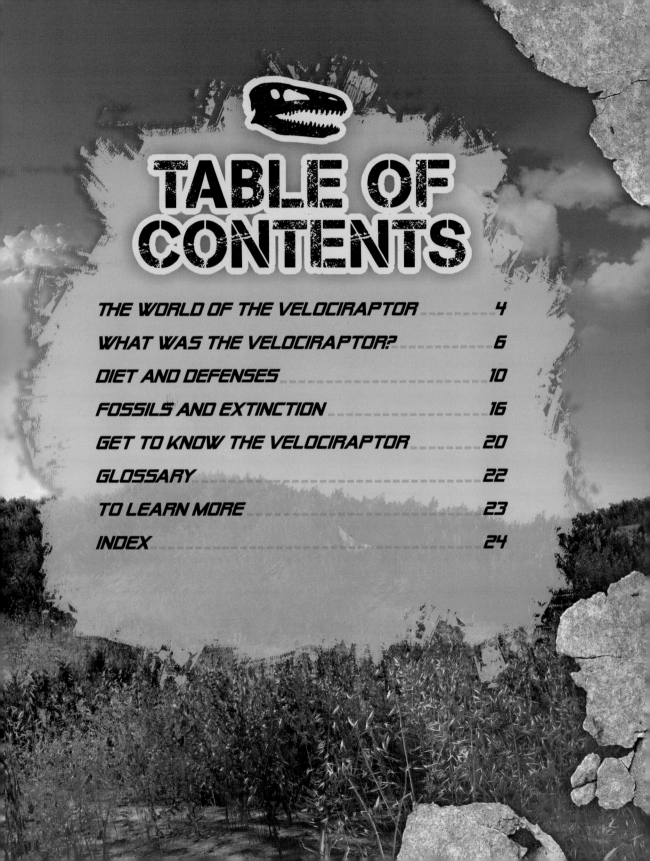

TABLE OF CONTENTS

THE WORLD OF THE VELOCIRAPTOR

The velociraptor was a deadly dinosaur! It is known for its sharp claws.

The dinosaur lived around 70 million years ago. This was during the Late **Cretaceous period**.

MAP OF THE WORLD

Late Cretaceous period

PRONUNCIATION

veh-LOSS-ih-RAP-tor

WHAT WAS THE VELOCIRAPTOR?

The velociraptor stood less than 2 feet (0.6 meters) tall. It weighed around 15 pounds (7 kilograms). The dinosaur was much like today's birds. It had feathers. Its bones were **hollow**. But the velociraptor could not fly!

SIZE CHART

	15 feet (5 meters)
	10 feet (3 meters)
	5 feet (2 meters)

⚠️ **ONE SMART DINO!**

The velociraptor had one of the largest brains of any dinosaur!

This dinosaur was built to be quick. It ran up to 24 miles (39 kilometers) per hour!
The velociraptor had a long tail. It helped the dinosaur stay balanced while making quick turns!

DIET AND DEFENSES

The velociraptor hunted at night.
Some scientists believe it hunted in **packs**.
This dinosaur had a great sense of smell.
It easily tracked down small dinosaurs.

NIGHT SIGHT

Scientists believe the velociraptor could see as well as an owl!

VELOCIRAPTOR DIET

small mammals

lizards

rotting meat

This dinosaur did not hunt down every meal. It was also a **scavenger**.

The velociraptor ate whatever meat it could find! It even ate the eggs of other dinosaurs.

The dinosaur had sharp claws to sink into **prey**. A special curved claw on each foot did extra damage.

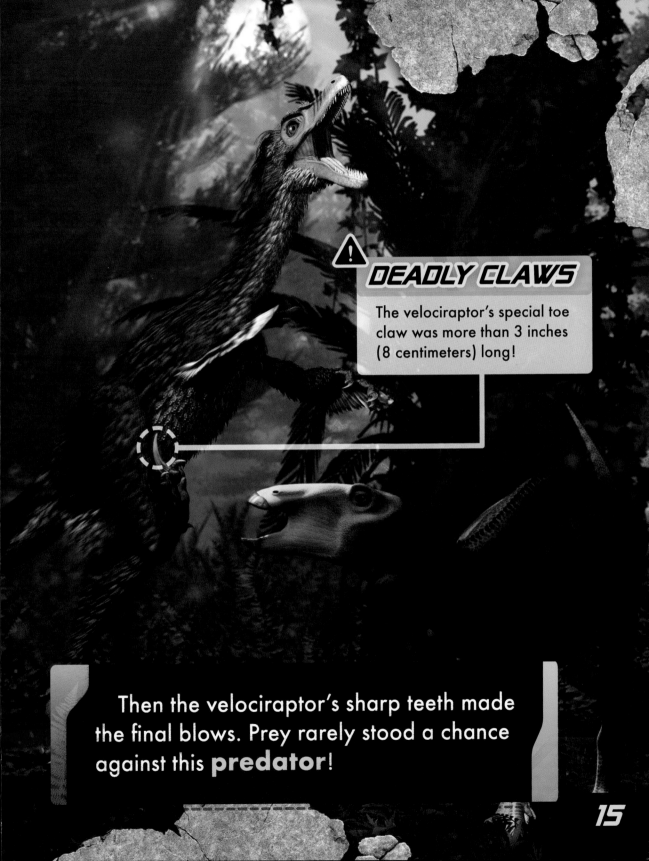

⚠ DEADLY CLAWS

The velociraptor's special toe claw was more than 3 inches (8 centimeters) long!

Then the velociraptor's sharp teeth made the final blows. Prey rarely stood a chance against this **predator**!

FOSSILS AND EXTINCTION

The velociraptor became **extinct** around 66 million years ago.

CRACKING THE WISHBONE MYSTERY

Birds need wishbones to fly. A wishbone was found in a velociraptor skeleton. This shows that birds may have come from dinosaurs!

Scientists found the first velociraptor **fossils** in 1923. But others have been found since then. The fossils teach us about the life of the velociraptor!

Scientists use new technology to uncover more about the velociraptor. They study bones to learn how the velociraptor lived.

velociraptor fossil

VELOCIRAPTOR FOSSIL MAP

Kazakhstan

Mongolia

Kyrgyzstan

Uzbekistan

Tajikistan

China

KEY

fossil site

More mysteries of the velociraptor may soon be discovered!

GET TO KNOW THE VELOCIRAPTOR

long tail

HEIGHT up to 2 feet (0.6 meters) tall

⚠️ **WEIGHT** around 15 pounds (7 kilograms)

🦖 **=** 🦃

⚠️ **FIRST FOSSILS FOUND**

1923 in Gobi Desert, Mongolia

sharp claws

LENGTH less than 6 feet (2 meters) long

⚠️ **LOCATION**

Asia

feathers

⚠️ **FOUND BY**

Peter Kaisen

⚠️ **FOOD**

lizards

small mammals

GLOSSARY

Cretaceous period—the last period of the Mesozoic era that occurred between 145 million and 66 million years ago; the Late Cretaceous period began around 100 million years ago.

extinct—no longer living

fossils—the remains of living things that lived long ago

hollow—empty through the middle

packs—groups of the same animals; velociraptors may have hunted in packs.

predator—an animal that hunts other animals for food

prey—animals eaten by other animals for food

scavenger—an animal that eats food that is already dead

TO LEARN MORE

AT THE LIBRARY

Gilbert, Sara. *Velociraptor*. Mankato, Minn.: Creative Education, 2019.

Grack, Rachel. *Discovering Velociraptor*. Mankato, Minn.: Amicus, 2019.

Peterson, Sheryl. *Velociraptor*. Lake Elmo, Minn.: Focus Readers, 2018.

ON THE WEB

FACTSURFER

Factsurfer.com gives you a safe, fun way to find more information.

1. Go to www.factsurfer.com.

2. Enter "velociraptor" into the search box and click 🔍.

3. Select your book cover to see a list of related web sites.

INDEX

The images in this book are reproduced through the courtesy of: James Kuether, front cover, pp. 4-5, 6-7, 8-9, 10-11, 12-13, 14-15, 16-17; Warpaint, p. 11 (small mammal); ZUMA Press, Inc/ Alamy, pp. 18-19; Herschel Hoffmeyer, pp. 20-21.